Through Painted Words

Artwork and words by Coralia Vallas

Order this book online at www.trafford.com
or email orders@trafford.com

Most Trafford titles are also available at major online book retailers.

Printed in the United States of America.

ISBN: 978-1-4907-0634-4 (sc)
ISBN: 978-1-4907-0633-7 (e)

Trafford rev. 08/03/2013

www.trafford.com

North America & international
toll-free: 1 888 232 4444 (USA & Canada)
fax: 812 355 4082

The Proverbial Child

This book is dedicated to

My Father

Thank you

This book is a collection of words written through many seasons of my life. I would like to thank those that stood by me and endured my seasons of change

This poem is for all of you

Whispers of delight dance in my mind
Shadows pass through the hands of time
You stood by me through night, through day
Encouraging hope along the way

You did not judge, you took my hand
Whispering of love, when I could not stand
Laughing together you wiped my tears
Standing by me throughout the years

You taught me to laugh and poke fun at myself
When lost in my thoughts and quiet as a mouse
You lifted me from the depths of despair
Simply by being you and always being there

When I stumbled and fell into the abyss
You came to me, even some with a kiss
You taught me to sing, even in the night
You accepted me and my wings took flight

Introduction

Poetry is an art. It has depth much like a painting. The viewer may admire the painter's work. But do they know the heart of the painter? I write poetry as a release of my heart. My hope is that through this book you can know a bit more of my heart. If my poetry touches a part of you and you are blessed let it be. I will call you my brother and hopefully you will call me your friend.

Table of Contents

Seeds In The Wind

The Poet

Innocently, I come to you
Traveling deep within my heart
Searching hidden caves
Seeking precious treasure
Gold burnished
By the tears of my sorrows
I give you my words
For they are all I have
To give
Words
Lived of my flesh
Born of my spirit
Breathed by others
Thoughts unsaid
Unseen faces
Strangers to my flesh
Yet, brothers to my soul

The Waterfall

The tears of my soul
Fill me up
Bottled
Denied within myself
They overflow
Creating a waterfall
Into the ocean
Unable to contain them
Any longer
The words
Like water
Pour from my lips
Violently gushing
From the spout of my mouth
Tears of joy and sorrow
Felt deep within the walls of my heart
The current pulling them out of me
Against my will, getting stronger and stronger
Shameless, I let go
The dam bursts
The walls turn to rubble
With laughter I ride the waves
Overwhelmed of the spirit
I savor the sweet release
As the tears become flesh
And I ask myself
Will they drink my tears or will it drown them
Will it quench their thirst or become poison upon their lips
As I ride the waves, I no longer care
For I am free

My Beloved

Where are you, my beloved
Are you sleeping beneath the shrubs
Or laughing in the treetops
You tantalize me with whispers in the night
And awaken me with music of your love
I am your weakness
And you are my strength
Do you laugh at my follies
As I search for you
You kiss me and run and hide
And I seek you
Why do you tease me
Are you testing my love for you
As you sing to me from beyond
I harken to your voice
I long to touch you
But cannot
If only for a moment
And you're gone
Oh how you taunt me in the night
Enticing me with your whispers
Seducing me with your smiles
I chase you
And I stumble
You reach for me
And you're gone
A spirit in the night
A flame amidst the darkness
One spirit
One eye

My Christ

As the moon beckons me
Such is my Christ
For in my darkest hour
He comes to me
A soft whisper in the night
An encouraging word
Beckoning me home
Through the shadows of despair
I see my Christ
An array of light
Amidst the evening silhouette
Radiating warmth within my being
Fond remembrance of yesteryear
His eyes caress my soul
As He carries a child upon His shoulders
Heavenly tenderness
A message of hope
As the darkness fades,
His light absorbs me
Cleansing my spirit
Open your eyes
It was not an illusion
The beauty still exists
The darkness was but a shadow
Remember yesterday with joy in your heart
For the Master was simply pruning you
For greater love
Our journey is not finished

It has only begun
Awake, little child, and place a smile upon your lips
And you shall see the light amidst the darkness
You are not alone
Arise, and walk with me
And you shall see the glory in the clouds
Do not be afraid any longer
Listen to the wind
And learn of the Spirit
And the Truth shall make you free

Angelic Freedom

As I walk upon the earth
How can it be
That who I remember
Is what I've become
Am I merely an extension
Of the earth
Nay, for I am
But a daughter of the moon
Soaring among the clouds
Reaching unreachable heights
Come fly with me
Look down upon the earth and smile
For in the clouds
The highest mountain
Cannot touch me
Les I swoop down
And chose to touch it
Laugh with the children
Of the earth
Wipe the tears
From their eyes
Yet do not seek
To become like them
Les my heart become heavy
And hinder my flight
For how is a bird
To walk amidst the earth
Ever so slowly
But in the clouds
She soars

And how am I to
Lead the broken hearted
With heaviness in my heart
But rather let me soar among the clouds
Beckoning them upward
Remember your Father
The Father of Time
Come fly with me
Let us meet together in the clouds
And dream a dream
Of home

Father of Time

Let not my mouth
Judgeth my brother
For who am I
But a mere mortal
Walking amidst the path
In search of my own destiny
And who is to know
Whether my brother
Walks amidst the same path
But the Giver of Life Himself
For is not He the one
Who searches a man's heart
And sees beyond the
Shadows of darkness
For isn't the darkness
Simply a veil
Blinding the man for a time
And a time
And a time again
And is not the Father of Time
Seerer of all things
Knoweth the beginning
And the end
For did He not say
I am the First
And the Last
Let me not cast
A stumbling block
Before my brother
As he walks amidst the night
Let my lips be silent
And spirit gentle
Harkening him home

The Wildflower

Blessed are the little children
For there in lies the heart of God
As they enter into the world
The remembrance of home
Fresh in their hearts
Trusting
Naive
A songbird amidst the darkness
Soaring
Free
Unknowing
Seeking beauty
Seeking love
Eyes open
Full of wonder
Are they not here for a purpose
Such as I
As I gaze into their eyes
I see a mirrored image
Of my soul
In another time
A wildflower
Growing amidst the weeds
Seeking the sun
Needing the rain
Growing forever upward
Yearning for the warm touch
Of the clouds
Let my heart become
As a little child
So as to soar with them
And not to encumber their precious flight

The Wild Rose

She was born on a cold winter's day
As the shadows of twilight bid farewell
And the first rays of the sun christened the skies
Life contained within a seedling
Nestled itself within the turbulent nature
And snow blanketed the earth
For many days and nights
It lay dormant beneath the snow
And the seasons changed
The clouds shifted in the heavens
As the Sun moved closer towards nature
And the earth beckoned to it's call
The snow turned to rain
As the earth drank in it's tears
And the soil became fertile
The seedling lay barren upon the earth
As without reason, it brought forth no root
And the soil became dry
Fruitless and alone
As it lay sterile upon the earth
The forces of nature smiled
And twilight danced in the skies
As the Wind rustled His wings
And caught the seedling in His arms
Boldly, it traveled amidst the night
As it lay nestled in the arms of the Wind
And it gazed upon the shadows of the earth below
The dark clouds diminished

As the Sun gave forth Her light
And the Wind became tired and died
Suddenly, the seeding dropped from the sky
As it violently impacted upon the earth
And was caught by the moist soil below
It struggled within the grip of the strange soil
As it reverently gave forth root
And joyously she began to grow within the earth
Her roots mingled with others
As she intertwined with weeds and flowers
An she grew strong and deep within the earth
On an enchanted afternoon
As the Sun radiated in the spring
She felt the warmth within her womb
She brought forth Life
As her leaves sprouted to the surface
And she became a plant
Passionately, she began to reach for the sky
As her leaves ached to touch the warmth of the Sun
And her stem grow strong bringing forth more Life
The Heavens became heavy and let down their tears
And it glistened upon her leaves as she drank in their moisture
Her thirst was quenched
The weeds watched her commune with the Heavens
As she responded to their call and was blessed without measure
And they seethed with jealousy
Their envy ran torrid through their stems, filling their roots
As they lurked closer towards her
And sought to kill her
Sadly, she looked upon the weeds

As she brought forth her thorns
And quickly they shrank from her
Fearless, she grew tall
As she overlooked the meadow
And drank in the splendor of nature
She laughed with the Wind
As He kissed her leaves
And she thanked Him with her growth
The scarlet blossom opened towards the sun
As the rose gave forth her magnificent beauty
And she wore her thorns as a crown upon her head
As a memento of her struggle within the earth

The Path

As I walk along the dark path
Crawling on my knees, for I have stumbled
With a tear stained face and an anguished heart
Groping for the ground beneath my feet
Tired and alone, confused by the shadows of darkness
Praying for deliverance, but knowing none
I feel the presence of someone walking towards me
Vaguely, I see a hand reaching for me
Is this the hand that will pull me to my feet
Or will it lead me deeper into the depths of the night
And how am I to know, for my journey through the night has been long and tiresome
I have stumbled against the rocks, and my wounds are still open
Deep wounds that bleed with tears unshed
Am I truly alone or has my own pain blinded my eyes
To others that walk the same path
Are they fellow travelers such as I
And how am I to know, les I get close enough to look into their eyes
And touch their wounds
Will I discover that they have stumbled against the same rocks
And suffered the same blows
That left scars upon their own flesh
And if I get even closer yet, to look inside their broken hearts,
Will I not discover the light within the shattered remains
Of a shell that once covered their hearts
A light that flesh cannot touch, les we choose to imprison it
With the walls that we ourselves create
Is not my own fear and anger
Which gives birth to these walls, which imprison my soul?

And truly I say, is not this the same light
Which I need to light my own path
Have I blinded my own eyes
Let not my grief harden my heart
For I do not wish to walk amidst the night
Gladly, I grasp the hand that reaches for me
Through the shadows, I see the palm
A deep scar
My Christ, come to rescue me
Pulling me to my feet, I gaze upon his face
A flame amidst the night
His warmth enfolds me
He lights my torch and I can see
His eyes beckon me to follow Him
As we walk, I glance from side to side
We are not alone
Hordes of souls, walking amidst the same dark path
Some walking fearlessly, yet blindly through the night
Stepping unknowingly upon the fallen ones and laughing
And others with their torches brightly lit
Kneel down to the blind which crawl upon the ground
Stumbling upon one another
Blind moles walking through tunnels that they themselves create
Some badly beaten, their wounds bleeding
Unable to dodge the swift footsteps of the fearless
Tears moisten my eyes
Overwhelmed
My brothers
Their pain, like blood, courses through my veins
In the distance, by the edge of the path
I see a small child hiding beneath the shrubs
Frail and hungered, weeping quietly

Others walk past carrying their torches
The hidden one goes unnoticed
For a quick moment, I forget the safety of my Lord
And run to the child and reach for him
Gladly, he grasps my hand
And the light within my heart burns brightly
I enfold him in my warmth
And pick him up and carry him
Slowly, I turn to look upon my Lord
An eternal flame across the path
A smile creeps upon His lips
And He walks on

The Ocean

To you, love of my flesh
Trampler of my words
Callously, you pour salt
Upon my wounds
You drink my blood
And spit upon my spirit
Why do you seek to destroy
That which you do not see
Am I not spirit
As well as flesh and blood
Why do you look upon the ship
And care nothing for ocean beneath
For who truly directs it's course
Is it the captain of the ship
Or the Hand that holds the ocean
For is not the ship at the mercy of the ocean
And yet, you admire the ship
The mahogany wood,
The crisp white sails
The freshly polished deck
Pouring your waste into the ocean
You pollute it
Insulting the Hand that created it
And why
Do you not understand
How can it be
A lover of my flesh
And hater of my spirit
For is not my flesh

Simply an extension of my spirit
As my words are an extension of my heart
Do you not see the wounds you inflict
Nay, for to see the wounds
You must search the ocean
Yet, you simply look upon the ship
That sails across the surface

The Wolves

You come to me as gentle sheep
Seeking to seduce me with your sweet perfume
You feed me honey
Made from bees
Which you keep locked away
In the dark cellars of your hearts
Busy bees, mechanically working
Building, creating
Planting seeds and giving birth
To a bigger swarm
And when you go to the dark cellar
To fill your cup with honey
Proudly made from your own hives
With your own labors
Angry and imprisoned
They turn on you
They swarm about you
And sting you
The sweet perfume
Turns to poison
Seeking to kill and destroy
That which God created
You call me your brother
Yet you seek to make me your slave
Imprisoning my heart
With your fears
And vexing my spirit
With your doctrines

But why
Is it because you cannot see
Beyond the bars that you create
Have you been locked away so long
That the darkness and the stench of the walls
Fills your nose and blinds your eyes
Do you not see that the honey
Though sweet upon your lips
Soon turns to blood
And the more you drink
The sicker you become
My anger turns to pity
I must flee you
But yet with a tear in my eye
Longing for you to be my brother
My heart swells and I want to reach for you
Yet cannot
For you shall pull me into your prison
And lock me away
And how is a man to walk amidst the dirty cellar floor
Once they have felt the grass beneath their feet
Do you think me proud
For I have been imprisoned
And felt the heaviness of their chains
I have been scorched and whipped
By the sword of thy mouth
And I have tasted blood upon my own lips
And seen the blindness in my own eyes
I have wept in the darkness and pleaded for deliverance
I have felt your pain

And I have seen the sunshine
And felt the warmth of His light
Why do you seek to cast me in the darkness
For to go back would be a certain death for me
The darkness would consume me
And would wither away and die
For the scars are still fresh
And the wounds have not healed
I must soak in the sun
And drink in the rain
And let my Lord refresh my soul
And heal my heart
And once again I shall walk
Unencumbered by chains of the past
And we shall be free
Together
Him and I

Whispers In The Dark

Divine Madness

Dialect of an Ancient tongue
Divine madness, my heart sung
Dance to the muse with Thee
Bewitching my soul with poetry
A gentle caress upon my mind
Spoken desires, wrapped in rhyme
Wickedly, you stole my heart
A thief within this precious art
Relentless, you embrace my soul
Captivating spirit, complete control
Surely, insanity has taken me now
Reason and Seasons, I cannot avow
Yet, within the divinity of madness
This Cheshire smile holds no sadness

Awaiting Sunrise

Awaiting warm kiss of the sun
To melt the chains of the day
Walking on sunbeams he sings
Whispering nuances they play
Beckoning farewell midnight
No shadows wrapped in words
Alone, souls rest in creation
Nature's angels, music of birds
Awaken, my love, to music
To the tune within your heart
Bound freely, one can dance
Walking together, while apart

Soul Mates

My dearest beloved
Danced in the night
Handing me stars
To hold till twilight
Christmas candles
To warm my heart
To light each day
We walked apart
A piece of heaven
Wrapped in hope
You gave to me
To help me cope
Golden stardust
Fell to the earth
Hole in my pocket
Formed at my birth
Creating a path
From me to you
Sprinkled in Light
As morning's dew
Where two hearts
Shall beat as one
In twilight's hour
After the sun

French Kiss

In the shadows
Devout of light
Dreams are formed
In thy darkest night
Entwined in rhymes
And rhythm and lore
Silent muse awakens
As lips crave more
Deep ebony eyes
Blanket the moon
Glimmers of stars
Fill nature's cocoon
An alluring flame
To warm thy heart
With destiny veiled
Mystery becomes art
As youth dance free
To the tune of thy soul
Within this embrace
I shall now bestow
That within the light
One can never dismiss
The beauty that lies
Within the French kiss

The Sun and the Moon

How can I compare Thee
To the sun and the moon
The day I met you
On that sad afternoon
My mind, a storm
With thoughts of death
Yet in your eyes
My soul could rest
A strange comfort
Welled up inside
At home with you
I could confide
How can I compare Thee
To the sun and the moon
The night you kissed me
My heart sang a tune
Not loud and boisterous
But gentle and sweet
Like the taste of your lips
My heart could keep
Visions of you
Danced in my mind
A song created
By the hands of time
How can I compare Thee
To the sun and the moon

The night you touched me
My body did swoon
To a far away land
The Muse spoke of
Existing in tales
Of dreamers in love
Where knights prevail
And maidens are fair
I sing you this song
Beloved, you're there
Thee is the sun
As I am a flower
Needing your touch
With each waking hour
At twilight I sleep
With you in my heart
Thee is the moon
The light in the dark

Destinee

Releasing the Muse
To dance before Thee
As shadows prance
In sheer revelry
Singing a tune
As freedom reigns
A carefree heart
Devout of chains
Gazing at stars
In cloudless skies
Lifting the spirit
Within your eyes
As children believe
In faeries and elves
Earth's magic revealed
Within themselves
Let faethe above
Reign on Thee
Catching the heart
Of your Destinee

Wisdom of Madness

Has wisdom become the result of great loss
Is the shadow of marked innocence the cost
Is it better to have truly loved and then lost
Where's the way back through brush and moss
Fallen knees, with a tear remembering a time
With a child's wonder my heart was a rhyme
Muses danced joyfully and playfully in mind
Not gloom or sorrow my soul would find
Mere madness has taken my heart and soul
As a cup of wisdom my mouth shall bestow
Drink up and quench your thirst as you sow
Worry not, for in your spirit your love shall grow
When love once again knocks at your door
Fluttering in your soul as your feet leave the floor
Soar in the clouds, even as you did before
Yet, fly higher this time and give all the more
For in your heart the child shall always live
If you refuse to give up and choose to give
Let your love be as grains of sand in a sieve
Shining through your heart, choose to forgive

Tempest Midnight

Painted words, whispers of delight
Shadows dance, tempest midnight
Within my mind, the words take form
The raging waters of desire is born
In darkness, the Muse sings a song
Silence no longer, whispers dawn
The soul awakens, the spirits soar
Shadows fade, within gypsy lore
Twilight awakens mocking the sun
Smiling temptation, the day undone
Yet laughing in darkness, life is born
No longer a slave to the light of the morn
Beauty unveiled, I dance in moonlight
A talisman, discovered beneath starlight
Breaking the chains, threatening sunrise
Releasing hope, beneath starlit skies

Morning Glory

Farewell to midnight's darkness
Cloaking the stars within the skies
Soft candles upon mere mortals
As secret dreams they surmise
Awakening the mornings glory
As periwinkle petals softly part
Welcoming the song of dawn
Dancing within nature's heart
Whispering music to the wind
As shadows cease to abide
Caressing the light of daybreak
Entwined in beauty, lovers hide
Each day brings a new creation
As flowers begin to bloom
Bringing Hope to mortal men
As the butterfly leaves her cocoon

Awakening Destinee

Whisper farewell sunset
While smiling at the moon
Dance within the shadows
As nature plays the tune
Gaze upon God's candles
Held by angels from above
Laugh within creation
Yet, as gentle as a dove
Stroke her hair at midnight
Soft kiss upon her cheek
Awake this sleeping beauty
Unravel her mystique
For in shadows she awaits
Relishing revelry
This fiery maiden you call
Catching your Destinee

The Quest

Yea heart yearns to trust
Yea soul desires to lust
But love is the quest
That allows the mind to rest
A gentle touch
Awakens so much
Yea mind protests
Yet the soul suggests
Release from tyranny
By self imposed misery
What is the word love
If not soft as a dove
Gentleness is its mark
The soft sound of a lark
Not forceful and violent
But gentle and pliant
Can yea heart still trust
When the rain turns to rust
That which was strong
Now seems so wrong
The poet sings songs
As yea heart still longs
For the kiss of a dove
The awakening of love
Dance if you must
In the song of my bust
But yea tread softly
And be not lofty
For it is my heart
Yea carry in a cart

Shadows In The Night

The Sleeping Poet

The poet along a dusty path
A frail old man
His limbs mere twigs
Brittle with age
His breathing now labored
From his long journey
He no longer hungered
To sustain his life
Death would be his friend
Carrying him home
To a place beyond the horizon
His lips dry and parched
Parted into a smile
As a twinkle lit in his soul
The Promised Land
He closed his eyes
He rested with the vision of home
Lifting a finger
He dropped a seed to the ground
He turned
To gaze upon the path he walked
Seeds filled the path
Still on the surface

A tear slid from the old man's eyes
Who would plant them?
Would the sun dry them up?
He closed his eyes
Moving forward
His bones aching
With faith
Embraced by his Maker
A peace engulfed him
And his quest
Was done

Hemlock

Quietly she fights a battle
She's determined to win
Battle marks of needles
Bruises upon skin
The shadow of Death
Knocks at the door
Whispering seductively
Give up the war
She closes her eyes
To struggle within
Looks Death in the face
You shall not win
A cocky smile
She invites him to dine
Death accepts the invitation
He smiles over wine
Together they drink
Challenging one another
For the wine is bitter
A poison, like no other
Soon drunken on wine
Death continues to drink
She slowly watches
Death come to his defeat
As she becomes weak
Her bones begin to ache
Visions flash before her
Yet, she is still awake

A perpetual ring
Persistent in ear
Hair falls to ground
As she looks in the mirror
She tries to stand
Her legs now weak
Metallic taste of food
She cannot speak
She stops drinking
Closes her eyes
Surely, it was enough
To bring Death's demise

Tattered Roses

When midnight came that hallow night
You closed your eyes, refused to fight
The music stopped, the silence came
No more tears, no more pain
Visions of yesterday
Dance in my mind
Your smile before me
Untouched by time
A laughing child
Youthful and glee
Who would of known
You would leave me
Daring and Bold
Adventure you sought
Gentle and carefree
Yet you fought
A battle known
Only to you
Alone you fought
No one knew
The struggle within
The fight to live
The darkness came
You could not give
To dreams of Hope
You could not run
Tattered roses
Need the Sun
When midnight came that hallow night
You closed your eyes, refused to fight

The music stopped, the silence came
No more tears, no more pain
Today I mourn
In the light of day
I remember the night
You were taken away
Hiding in shadows
My tears form words
As I screamed No
To be heard by birds
Broken, defeated
Midnight came
Inside my heart
Beneath the pain
Today a void
Is left behind
In my heart and soul
Untouched by time
I miss your spirit
I miss your song
I miss the day
You walked strong
To dreams of Hope
You could not run
Tattered roses
Need the Sun
When midnight came that hallow night
You closed your eyes, refused to fight
The music stopped, the silence came
No more tears, no more pain

Wrinkles of Wisdom

For in the midnight hour, Death whispered to me
Binding my heart's desire, no chance to be free
To believe in tomorrow, of memories to come
As young knave of yesteryear, could no longer run
From the battles he fought, beneath the Sun's rays
The tempest night destroyed him and he ended his days
As maidens still grieve under the light of the moon
Remembering the night he came to his doom
Yet, within Life's storm, an angelic being was formed
Not of flesh and blood, but a spirit transformed
Enshrouded in Grace, surely his spirit does grow
Under the shield of his Creator, his wings now glow
Lighting the candles, held by the souls of men
A guardian angel now lives, a brother and a friend
Wrinkles of wisdom, cast upon his young face
Shadows on the face of Time, healed by God's Grace

The Guardian

To respect the memory of the dead
And those that have gone before
Past the shadows among this life
To a place where love is pure
My heart soars above the darkness
As a beacon shines within the night
Your strength shall guide my journey
As I walk the earth, my wings ignite
For an angel now walks within me
An endearing comfort from above
A sweet and fragrant memory
Of merciful and unconditional love
Illuminating the long path before me
Embracing each step of the way
For I shall no longer walk in darkness
But rather in the brilliant light of day

The Forgotten Soldier

When midnight came
Within his heart
The forgotten soldier
Choose to depart
A shadow remains
Within the grave
The forgotten soldier
No one could save
His memory still lives
A beacon of light
An angel of mercy
For those who fight
Carrying them home
To a place of peace
Shedding their armor
No swords of cerise
By night and morn
Awaits his quest
To comfort the soul
That seeks rest

The Tempest Sea

Thy wings of thy storm
Beat against thy sea
Creating understanding
Deep within me
Waves of wisdom
Form in the deep
Beneath thy surface
Life will reap
Thy soul eternal
In the hands of Time
Continues to grow
As thy clocks will chime
On the surface
Nature brings thy rain
Yet Life's journey
Is beneath thy pain
Nature's great fury
May touch thy soft flesh
Yet, thy spirit is a bird
Untouched in a nest
Thy comfort of God
Lives in the deep
Open thy eyes
To the beauty and reap
For it is not shame
Casting tears to soil
It is thy love
Nature cannot spoil

Sing Loudly, Little Angel

A sweet little angel came to me today
Smiling, she told me of her plans to stay
She wanted to walk upon mortal earth
Opening heavenly gifts from her birth

Helping those that walk in the night
A counselor of hope, a beacon of light
To become the wind beneath their wing
She sought to dance, she sought to sing

Her dream was to help those who now cry
That walked the same path beneath the sky
To comfort those that had once felt abuse
She sought to go to school so to be of use

As glimmers of hope danced upon her face
I gazed at this child, now a woman of grace
I held her in my arms as she said goodbye
Grateful to feel her wings beneath the sky

Yet, God had a different plan for her tonight
Bringing her home to be His angel in flight
Dancing in clouds, she sings with great joy
In the realm of angels, man cannot destroy

Sing loudly, little angel so mortals can hear
The beauty of your soul both far and near
Comforting those that walk in the night
Sweet little angel, golden wings ignite

Forgotten Lark

When the sun whispers farewell to the day
And the robins call bids the winds to take leave
Silence comes in the heart of the aching moon
As lanterns cleave to skies, then ye soul grieves

Not in bustling of the exchanging of spirit vows
When the poet dance in words of nature's hue
Blossoming to a rose within the cardinal's breast
As delicious laughter feeds upon the nature's dew

Rather, it comes in waves upon a lonesome sea
As a siren settles in the empty tomb of thy heart
Dark reminiscent clouds, a shroud upon the horizon
Love's unmet thirst, the lyrics of the forgotten lark

The Bay of the Moon

Deep ebony shadows of thy blackest night
Threaten the lighthouse on the bay of the moon
As a sea of weeping stars cradle the faded skies
A lonely siren sings, haunting the earth's groom

"I love thee" she sang to mountains of yesteryear
When lanterns filled the skies, the moon ever clear
A dance of one she sings, embraced only by the wind
"If only", a daunting command she could not rescind

Solace

I dance to the music deep within lakes of my soul
A comforting embrace, unseen hands, my counsel
Longing for the touch of one, who can understand
The whispers of my heart, in the form of a man

The solace gesture of one to unburden my heart
To breathe the breath of faith, when torn apart
A docile soul with the strength of a concrete man
To open the eyes of my heart, to live once again

A Poet Lost

If you see me whispering in the shadows of the night
Beneath the ebony skies, would you hold me so tight?
If you see my walking alone along the lonely shore
Would you take my hand, walk with me forevermore?

If you see me in the empty crowds of the day's sweet bliss
Would you remember I am a woman in need of a kiss?
If you see me carrying a heavy burden upon my shoulder
Would you share my burden, as the weather gets colder?

If you see all my imperfections in both night and in day
Would you forgive me as I stumble on words I can't say?
If you see me tremble when I become lost and alone
Would you be my lighthouse and bring me to my home?

The Face of the Storm

The storm has passed
And the rainbow has come
The earth has been quenched
Nothing is left undone
In the wake of the storm
The trees were uprooted
Tears fell from heaven
As the earth was looted
Nature's great fury
Unleashed for a day
Poseidon was glorified
As Zeus sought to play
Mortals disheveled
As Hera did weep
Apollo was glorified
In the face of the deep
As the horses
Drove the sun
Aphrodite awakened
And all was done

Seasons Of The Soul

Tenacious Hope

Shadows of fear
Whisper to my heart
Yet tenacious Hope
Will not depart
For within this
Tender exterior
An iron will
Becomes superior
Shattering doubts
As pots of clay
A brazen Sun
On a cloudy day

The Birth of Wisdom

The birth of wisdom
Lives not in the dark night
When moon casts its glow
And whispers a solemn melody
Nor the breaking of the dawn
As the morning glories unfold
To the crimson song of the cardinal
Rather wisdom is heavily labored
On a path of shadows in hued grey
As twilight is formed in the mind
Intertwined in a lovers embrace
As ebony eyes gaze upon
Waking stars bursting forth
The heavens unfold
Shadows lost
Light

The Glass House

The adoring skies
The house on the hill
Stands in the valley
Seeking to kill
For within the walls
Illusions are birthed
The mad man believes
He will not be cursed
For he dreams to work
In a place ruled by men
Where security and riches
Will not have an end
Given a badge of honor
To work with the elite
Proudly he journeys
To the house of deceit
Within walls, I shall dance
Cloaked in man's security
Dreaming an endless latter
To a place of maturity
Where man honors talent
As creativity shall flow
Ambition shall rule me
In this lie, I bestow
To dream a dream
In the house of glass
Until the sun rises
Reality, alas

The shadows fade
In the morning's light
And all can be seen
Hidden in the night
Monkeys are trained
Within the glass wall
To sit at their desks
The cubicle, their stall
Simple tasks given
A fool can complete
Streamlining the dollar
The house is complete
Dispensable monkeys
In the house they surpass
To climb the latter within
To a ceiling of glass
As creativity is lost
And ambition destroyed
The monkeys within
Soon become annoyed
Outside man watches
The monkeys perform
A tear in his eye
In the face of the storm
Will the glass hold them
From nature's great wrath
Are they really protected
In a house made of glass

Springtime Friends

After the chill in the air, of the cold winter's blast
Springtime friends, whispering in the winds of the past
Adoring the earth with a beautiful blossom in a tree
These spirits come and go, a sweet fragrance to me
For a moment, they blossom within the season
Angelic spirits walking the earth, sent for a reason
To help one through a trial, to offer a helpful hand
To lift one's spirit, allowing one's soul to expand
Leaving footprints in the sand, that fade with time
Springtime friends vanish as nature's clock will chime
As flowering blossoms die, a fragrant memory remains
Springtime friends for a season, lifetime friends sustain
The elements of fierce nature, life's seasons of change
Beautiful blossoms may die, yet strong branches remain
As a soul grows upon the earth, as a tree in the ground
Springtime friends within season, lifetime friends abound
Through the shadows of winter, the early morning snow
Lifetime friends stand firm, for in their heart they know
More than a friend, they are formed as a branch to a tree
Lifetime friends, enduring seasons, become a part of me

Windows of the Soul

As the whispery winds beat against my house
The windows within my mansion hold a light
Warmth is captured within my home
The winds do not penetrate
My eyes reveal the kingdom within
Forever young, my eyes do not age
The walls of the castle may crumble
The shrubs which accent the home
May become overgrown
The sidewalks cracked with age
Yet, within my home my eyes reveal a kingdom
That grows stronger with each day
The child of long ago dances within these walls
Lovers intertwine in a passionate embrace
Songs like that of Psalms bounce against the walls
Filling the kingdom with music
As the enchanted room is filled with smiles
Joy is bountiful
It is all revealed in a twinkling of my eye
Let the kingdom stand
Till the shades be drawn
And the world become veiled to the light
As it dances in my eyes

A Sacred Gift

Between the silence of twilight and morn
Sweet blessings of God, pure Hope is born
A sacred gift, wrapped in the spirit of Joy
To understand Grace, through a small boy
Wisdom and Love were packaged within
This gift from God, breaking a chain of sin
That held souls captive, to a hopeless path
Self imposed tyranny and man's great wrath
Beloved Son of God, a candle in our night
Enlightening our souls, as a flame does ignite
Casting light on the darkness that we knew not
Planting seeds of Hope in our open heart
Transforming our spirits to walk as One
God's heavenly family beneath the Sun
A rainbow of rays, to light the Earth
An aura of praise, the aroma of mirth

One God

Visions of yesterday
Shadows in my mind
Scars upon my flesh
Encompassed by Time
As a new tomorrow
Awakens in the morn
The shadows pass
As Hope is born
Whispering sprites
Dance in delight
A song has begun
The embers ignite
To a world of peace
Within my soul
No longer troubled
The angels extol
To believe again
In Grace and Love
The virtues of God
Sent from above
As maidens dream
Of distant lands
Praying for peace
Within God's hands
As Faith is restored
In the hearts of man

To believe one God
A world without end
Devout of strife
Mourning and grief
Brothers and sisters
To share the belief
That they are one
Beneath God's Light
His beloved children
That walk in the night

Grace

When the shadows fade
And the storm has ceased
Will I walk among the living
Or travel with the deceased
Will dead man's bones
Fill the twisted path
That leads to heaven
Or God's great wrath
Yesterday's sunshine
Warming my face
Blinding my eyes
To God's great grace
Can I walk this path
Shall it lead me home
To a greater love
Than I have ever known
Forgiveness has come
In the face of a dove
Igniting my heart
To God's great Love
The jester laughs
Folly he sees
As I walk this path
In search of the keys
To unlock the doors
That imprison the soul
A treacherous journey

Through caves of a mole
Beneath the earth
Alone and dark
A fire in my heart
And the sound of a lark
Trust is a word
Spoken by few
Can it be reborn
In the morning's dew
Beneath the angels
And God's great Grace
His spirit shall comfort me
When I see His face

Masquerade

Mystery entered the ballroom
Her modest dress marked her innocence
Untouched as her soul she kept hidden behind
The mask that sealed her
Hungry, her spirit devoured the sparkle
Magic danced in the faceless crowd
Safely observing as eyes upon a distant shore
Until she was drawn
By the hands of a masked knight
Clothed in unseen armor
Only to be illuminated in darkness
As the strings of a guitar
Carefully intertwined within her soul
The artist stroked each chord to her heart
As the melody was birthed within the rhythm
And shadows danced upon waking walls
The delicate sound of the beloved melody
Could only be heard through veiled eyes
For senses are keen in darkness
And dreams are formed
Within shadows

He Whispered

Through eyes closed, He whispered
As the world shouted in a realm of chaos
As the brazen sun demanded justice
The clouds formed in the mind's eye
Threatening a jealous sky
As Poseidon's fist
Beat against
The deep
On a distant shore
The clouds parted, revealing
Welcoming rays upon untouched skin
As the wind tangled a rainbow of leaves
In her autumn hair she listened quietly
To the soft sound beyond the horizon
Communing with the Master of her soul
Within the dense walls of Hades
The iron chains of chaos grip thy soul
The gentle song of the lark cannot be heard
Within the bared cage with festers the mind
Yet, within the purity of the fresh fallen snow
Peace surrounds thy soul as a brilliant light
That engulfs thy spirit to dance freely
Alas, let the gods of nature reap havoc upon the earth
As they lust for power to devour the souls of men
Yet, in your humility let the wings of your soul
Rest unfettered, the Master whispered
Removing the leaves
Tangled in her autumn hair

The Blank Canvas

He stares at me
In his solitude
Seducing me
Yearnings
Of desire
Alone
He waits
In stillness
To fill the void
Of emptiness
I touch his face
The soft caress
Of my brush
Whispering
To dance
He smiles
His desire met
In unison, we embrace
To the song of color
Exploding
As one

Remember Me

When the ebony shadows dance
To the soft echo within your heart
And the ocean in your eyes
Crashes the shore in waves of tears
Remember me, as part of me forever
Still swims in the turbulent sea
At peace I am with you
As my skin is the salt
Of your tears
When the ominous clouds form
Threatening the horizon with rain
And the storm in your mind
Thunders into your voice
Remember me, as part of me forever
Still sings in the tempest sky
At peace I am with you
As my song is the rain
Of your whisper
When the sun awakens the shoreline
Promising a rainbow in a cloudless sky
And the rapture in your smile
At last washes your face
Remember me, as all of me forever
Now dances in angelic light
At peace I am with you
As my dance is in the warmth
Of your smile

Nature's Dance

Beyond Our View

Just beyond our view
Rainbow meets the sea
Hidden treasure found
Waiting for you, for me
Precious gold burnished
By the hour glass of time
Molten desires met
If you truly seek to find
Joy surpasses sorrow
In this golden paradise
Sleeping not in shadows
Letting your eye concise
The beauty of the view
Is seen from the eye within
With open doors of gratitude
Let the journey begin!

Sage

Colors of Sage
The wind whispered through my hair
Watercolors of petals painted air
Held by the hand of the wind
To cherish the beauty
I kept within
Open your eyes to colors of sage
A talisman within this fiery age
Held by the hand of the heart
To embrace the music
In forms of art

Ablaze

Eyes of deep coal
Burning with ember
Crimson passion ablaze
Of my heart's surrender
Hot liquid gold burning
Through the hour glass
Open the gates of fate
To true love, alas!

Awakenings

I ponder the words
Of love and loss
Musing awakenings
The heart, the cost
Without clothes
In a barren land
Hearts exposed
As sun on sand
Radiating warmth
Unable to burn
Tattered pages
Of love forlorn

Upon the Shore

Time for me to fly away
Open wings upon the shore
Feathers catch the wind
As feet leave sand forever more

Moments shared in time
Embraced within the heart
Imprints upon the soul
Residue of Cupids dart

Sorrow leaves the dream
Waiting upon the shore
As the ship embarks to travel
A new destiny forever more

With contentment, I could stay
Wrapped in the sands of time
Walking with you upon the shore
Leaving footprints of my heart behind

Yet, where would your desire be
As I commit my heart to you?
Would you search inside my eyes
To swim in oceans of emerald blue?

Poseidon's Kiss

Dear Grecian god of the sea
Alas! You stole his heart from me
A sailor's quest, a distant shore
A maiden's despair forever more

How can I compare thy soul to thee
Tempestuous mistress of the sea
Captivating a man's deepest desire
To seek adventures, a lady's mire

Damn Poseidon of the deep!
Seducing man, as widow's weep
Whispering within their ear
"The love of the sea is ever near"

The Sirens Song

The icicles of solemn winter
Drape walls upon my heart
The sharp knife of cold winds
Embrace the song of the lark

As a siren sings upon the seas
Calling men unto their doom
She speaks a lonely song to me
In the wake of the light of moon

Shadows prance, a carefree dance
In the distant shores of my mind
Alas! The welcomed dawn arise
To turn the broken page of time

Bittersweet

Bittersweet upon my tongue
Words reveal, a heart undone
Candied kisses, dance in mind
Deliciously untouched by time

Embers ignite in hungry eyes
Feeding memories, I surmise
Delightful feast within my soul
Devouring, lingering eyes of coal

A ravenous touch upon my heart
Embracing muse in forms of art
Quenching thirst of my reservoir
To parched lips with a metaphor

Brazen Moon

Remember the timid moon
When you gaze upon the sea
Whisper to her aching heart
In darkness, she guides thee

Alone, she walks in shadows
In comfort of a neighbor star
Clothed within the seasons
She loves you from afar

She is not cold to you
In the still of the night
Her heart is a brazen fire
Just as the sun's delight

Cherish the thoughts of her
As she holds you in her heart
Longing for you to know her
Never wishing to depart

Calopogon Orchid

Sweet Grecian wildflower
Unravel your petals of pink
Taunt me, you rugged beauty
Daunt me in your mystique

Whisper to me of your love
Let me revel in your deceit
Intoxicated by your scent
Drunken desire we meet

Lavish me with passion
As I think not of 'morrow
Awaken conversant muse
Quench me of my sorrow

The Sentinel

Once a fierce sentinel
Guarded her soft heart
Carrying a strong shield
Against Cupid's dart

Safely she could slumber
In Aphrodite's world
While dreaming of romance
Without her spirit unfurled

Each day the sentinel
Placed rocks near her heart
Till a strong wall formed
To keep her apart

The wall became a tomb
As sorrow her friend
Loneliness engulfed her
Till the bitter end

One night there was a clash
Lightning lit the sky
A fierce battle had formed
Through sentinel and nigh

The sentinel was killed
Through words of a knight
The wall now mere rubble
Tattered wings took flight

Warmly she could embrace
The piercing of her heart
No longer fearful
Of Cupid's sharp dart

Thy Heart's Mystery

To walk behind the curtain
That veils your soul from mine
Alas! What treasure awaits
Which painting shall I find?

A fragrant garden of roses
Leading to the gates of fate
A shallow stream of water
Of love that came too late

The mystery of thy heart
Held captive in your eyes
Tattered pages yet unread
Alas! The muse surmise

Dancing yet in shadows
Longing kiss of the dawn
Awaiting breath of life
Sleep now, love forlorn

Awake me yet 'morrow
Virgin love return to me
Open up morning flower
Let us dance in revelry

Taunt me with desire
Burn the hands of time
Whisper to me of love
Enchant me with a rhyme

Timid Moon

Gazing upon the crescent moon
Whispering softly in hues of blue
Intimately hugging his other half
Wrapped in the timid night
By candlelit stars
They sleep
As one
Till the scarlet passion
Awakens their restful sleep
Together they fade in the clouds
As the radiant sun chains the earth

Water Lily

Water lily dreams
In silence upon the crest
Floating Devoting
Beauty abreast
A seafaring maiden
Upon the gates of fate
Longing belonging
Life equate
Delicately strong
Resting upon nature's tide
Emerging urging
Trust abide

His Earth

Is she just another burning distant star?
Or a resilient lantern in a memorial sky
Nature splendors her spiritual procession
The aroma of reverent prayer her cry

As you reach for a hundred stars to touch
To fill the void within the temple's spire
Think upon the love of one surrendered
Destined to evolve around the sun's lair

She is your earth who orbits your heat
Your warmth the river to parched lips
A baby upon the breast of her mother
Reaching for you in a solar eclipse

Waves of Desire

Swollen lips crave more
Gentle kiss upon the shore
Waves of desire ache
Satin skin upon sea's quake

The tide releases the sea
To wash thy shore of thee
Till 'morrow brings thee home
Upon the sands fingers roam

Whispering in thy ear
"It is thy heart, ye shall not fear"
Building castles in the sand
Till 'morrow brings you to land

Captive Poetess

Can you understand
His alluring touch upon my hand?
Captivating my desire
To dance with words, in the fire

Alas! My love for thee
Is as boundless as an endless sea
Apollo! Shackle me
To Erato's sweet decree

Deliciously kind
In the dungeon of my mind
A brilliant light
Subsides thy darkest night

A tender kiss
Upon an oceanic abyss
Muse! Breathe unto me
Carry away my debris!

Evening's Vow

Crescent moon is smiling still
It's breath as dew drops of light
Upon the morning's glory bough
Petals of blue as lips untouched
Honoring the evening's vow
As bashful eyes turn aside
The flower gazes at the moon
Lovelorn eyes do surmise
Hope to return soon

The Tempo of Solitude

I dance in starlit clouds
The gypsy lore of my muse
In the rhythm of solitude
Shadows cannot confuse
The tempo of each string
Violin of my sacred soul
Tranquility, nature's song
Divine whispers console
Noise of neighbor's minds
Clamor upon my shore
Till the quake of the ocean
Washes sands forevermore

Temple of Sorrow

She built a temple
Strong walls to protect
Memoirs of his love
As she could reflect
Heavy storm clouds
Threaten blue skies
Dancing in her temple
Sorrow in her eyes
Clothes sodden
Upon her soft flesh
Infant in her soul
Her sacred crèche
Joy in her sorrow
Dancing in the rain
Unforgotten memoirs
Comforting her pain

The Twin Soul

Dew upon a rose
In dawn's early light
As tears in a garden
Caress the beauty
In the night
The moon and a tear
Entwined as one
As twin breasts
Upon the soul
Untouched by
The sun
Sweet delicacy
Of a feast
Devoured by two
A tear and a smile
Unquenched
Within you

A Blue Horizon

Misty eyes of a blue horizon
As the sky kisses the sea
In an intimate embrace
A tear and a smile
As clouds part
One become two
As the soul awakens
Upon a new destination
Yet the wet kiss of the rain
Remains in the heart of clouds

Welcomed Friend

Aye, the moon
Smiles in the heavens above
Whispering the verse in notions of love
Daybreak comes
Laughter in rays of light
Beauty's song, the flowering buds delight
Aye, the spring
My sweet welcomed friend
Awakening my senses to winter's end
Morning's glory
Sing a new song in petals of blue
Unleashing the soul freedom anew

Wings of Desire

Abandoned garden gates
Surrender to husky wind
As crimson petals ache
Hungry desire within
Passion burns as embers
Communion of the heart
Desires yet unmet
Ruffled wings of a lark

Latte Love

Coffee Kisses
Soft touch of rain
Innocent thoughts
Hearts entertain
Purity of children
Lost in the night
My silvery spoon
Of sweet delight

Heart Beguile

Dogwood blossoms
On this summer's eve
Out the window I gaze
My soul now at ease
Pondering the past
As a search the morn
Awaken by angels
Cold winter, forlorn
Shall I ever see, eyes
That made me smile
A touch that made me
Quake, heart beguile
If never shall see you
In the parting of day
Your memory I keep
Warm as a sun's ray

Kinship of the Muse

Words of angels
Comfort my soul
The beauty of art
As the spirit extol
Strangers to flesh
Inspire me, muse
Kinship to a soul
Healing my bruise
Yet, for now
I must depart
For I am lost
In sacred art
Alas, I must go
As mortals walk free
Farewell to a friend
That stood beside me

Love's Magic

Dancing in the dark
Singing as a lark
Whisper sacred winds
They are without sins

They are clothed in love
Feathers of a dove
Youthful innocence
Without bivalence

Who can then accuse
The scholar or muse
The simpleton agrees
Lovers hold the keys

Unlocking the doors
Between Life and wars
The hostage set free
From lore of banshee

My Beloved's Song

I shall seek the sun
That resides within my heart
An ember to my soul
An ardor that won't depart
Comforting my spirit
In a place untouched by man
Whispering to my muse
As an angel within my hand
As a pen upon a paper
His music in my ears
Dancing in forms of art
Releasing all my tears
My beloved's song
The essence of my soul
Forever he lives strong
As he did long ago
Resting in his wings
A lullaby was heard
An infant in his arms
The melody of a bird
As a child deep within
I heard him sing to me
My beloved's song
A sweet symphony

Unchartered Love

The warmth of naked feet
Buried securely in the sand
The sounds of ocean's quake
Arouse nature's siren upon land

"Awaken secret desire
Prisoner within thy mind
Alas! Dance with thee
Leave thy hurt behind"

As I heard her speak to me
Upon the troubled shore
My spirit listened curiously
To the wisdom in her lore

"Be not afraid to love
For love have no bounds
Rather embrace her soul
Till her spirit astounds"

I unburied my naked feet
And shook the sand free
I boarded my ship that day
In search of my destiny

Hungry Rain

When thy hungry rain comes
Trickling upon my soul
Washing away our thirsty time
Diminishing eyes of coal

I wait upon waking dawn
Arise to chain thy distant shore
Alas! My soul is free
To love forevermore

Open up thy crimson heart
For him to come to thee
To swim among the waves
Into my arm's destiny

Love's Birth

Is love formed within ebony skies?
In the edge of the hand of winter
Piercing the heart with a gust
Is love formed in grey shadows?
As evening bow meets twilight
And a gentle hand cradles the heart
Is love formed in birth of sunrise?
As music of birds awakens the song
Blossoming within the open heart

Love's Master

Is love the blaze of raging fire
Consuming the soul in madness
Burning the dual lens of clarity
Till ebony skies blanket the eyes
Chaining the indentured heart
To thy master of an unquenchable thirst?
Or is it a wild spark that ignites the coal to ember
Lifting the heart to ache with warmth
To the consummation of the lover of its soul
As water lily floats upon the river of its desire
Freely pulled by the undercurrent its own heart?

Eden

There was a peaceful garden
When Love first began
Fragrant flowers blossomed
Many colors of man
Each containing a beauty
Each entwined as one
A majestic rainbow
Reflecting the loving Sun
Unafraid we lived
To love one another
With our hearts exposed
We did not seek cover
We danced in the garden
To the sound of love
We saw the inner beauty
A gift from God above

Unclothed

I used to paint words in a metaphoric prose
Sorrow hidden in words, an unopened rose
As the moon shone upon shadows in night
Glimpse of my heart whispered in light

Alas! I come to speak to the spirit within
Opening thy petals, to live without sin
"Do not be afraid of what lies in the deep
It's the spirit of God, you shall not weep"

Now I paint through a rose colored lens
To a peace within, to a heart that mends
Singing with the angels for the earth to see
Unclothe thy light, and sing with me!

The Natural

She paints nudes with a child's eye
Embracing innocence where angels lie
Purity revealed within human form
Unclothed and natural, within Life's storm

The essence of a soul built in each shape
Representing the spirit we cannot escape
Free, unhindered she paints from her heart
A vulnerable nature she had from the start

If the viewer should look with beauty, not lust
He shall see a heart contained in the bust
She paints nudes with a child's eye
Embracing innocence where angels lie

Labors of Love

Ah! Awake
Chains of the day
Crimson horizon
Promises to stay
As a robin's call
Welcomes spring
Rejoice, my soul
New song to sing
Let me dance to
The muse in me
Labors of love
Pure revelry!

The Gift

I felt the salty mist dance upon my skin
I felt ocean quake trembling deep within
I felt the morning grass wet between my toes
I smelled the scent of roses fragrant to my nose

I made passionate love with the ocean's crest
I birthed a child, a mother's love within my breast
I danced within Life's fire, embraced by my friends
I lived a life of passion through a rose colored lens

When my ship embarks to sail, my soul has no regret
For the Master of this bough, thy sun shall never set
I danced within thy Light and shall live forever more
As I continue on my journey, upon the distant shore